POSY EDWARDS

LIAM HEMSWORTH

AGAINST ALL ODDS

Introducing LIAM!

"All the girls liked Liam," says school pal Laura Griffin. "He was popular, a bit of a joker, and made me laugh."

A talented actor with the whole world at his feet, Liam Hemsworth is on the way to becoming one of Hollywood's brightest stars. A tall, muscular Australian who is already getting big movie roles at the beginning of his career, Liam is set for great things after a whirlwind career that began with a role in the soap *Neighbours* when he was 17 years old.

Now, having scored a leading part in *The Hunger Games* and being offered some of the hottest scripts in Hollywood, Liam's become a pin-up the world over. Not bad for a guy who only took up acting because both his older brothers were doing it!

LIAM HEMSWORTH: FACT FILE

FULL NAME // LIAM HEMSWORTH

BORN // 13 JANUARY 1990

STAR SIGN // CAPRICORN

HEIGHT // 6ft 3in

SIBLINGS // TWO BROTHERS, CHRIS AND LUKE

HOMETOWN // HE WAS BORN IN MELBOURNE, AUSTRALIA, BUT GREW UP IN PHILLIP ISLAND (HOME TO THE PENGUINS... SUPER CUTE!)

CURRENT HOME // A LOS ANGELES APARTMENT WITH HIS BROTHER CHRIS

FIRST ROLE // A WALK-ON PART IN AUSTRALIAN SOAP *HOME AND AWAY* IN 2007

FAVOURITE SPORT // SURFING. HE OFTEN SURFS NEAR NEWPORT BEACH AND HUNTINGDON BEACH IN CALIFORNIA

FAVOURITE SPORTSPERSON // SURFER KELLY SLATER

FAVOURITE MOVIES // *THE DEPARTED*, *SUPERBAD*

FAVOURITE FOOD // SUSHI

JOB BEFORE HE BECAME AN ACTOR // LAYING FLOORS

CELEBRITY GIRLFRIEND // LIAM HAS DATED SINGER AND ACTRESS MILEY CYRUS ON AND OFF SINCE 2010

In the beginning...

Liam was born on 13 January 1990, in the Australian city of Melbourne, to mum Leonie and dad Craig Hemsworth. They already had two sons: eldest child Luke and Chris, who was born in August 1983. The family had originally settled in the remote Aboriginal community of Bulman in the Outback, so Luke and Chris were used to a rural life before their little brother came along.

"My earliest memories were on the cattle stations up in the Outback, and probably my most vivid memories were up there with crocodiles and buffalo," older brother Chris remembers life before Liam. "Then we moved to Melbourne and Liam came along."

It was there that the three brothers grew up and went to school, with youngest boy Liam spending his early years in the suburbs of the city, the second biggest in the whole of Australia. The boys got to ride the city's trams, watch the Dragon Boat racing at the Melbourne Docklands, and visit the Etihad Stadium that plays host to lots of sporting events including soccer, cricket, rugby and Australian Rules football.

"I'm the youngest so I've always looked up to my brothers and I was always influenced by what they were doing. Maybe I wouldn't have become an actor if my older brothers weren't actors, but now that I'm here, I really enjoy it and it's what I feel most comfortable doing."

SCHOOL DAYS

Life changed for the boys the year after Liam left primary school. The family decided to move away from Melbourne, so when he was 13 years old, their clothes and furniture were packed up and Liam, Luke, Chris and their parents moved to Phillip Island.

It was quite a change for them all. From the bright lights of big city Melbourne, they found themselves on an island that's 140km away from their former home. Linked to the mainland town of San Remo by a bridge, Phillip Island has only about 7000 people living on it – although the pretty island gets about 40,000 visitors during the summer. It was a beautiful – if quiet – place for Liam to grow up. There's a wildlife park full of wallabies and kangaroos and the island is famous for its Penguin Parade, where Little Penguins (the smallest type of penguin) come ashore in groups at dusk every night. Awww!

SURF'S UP

It was here that young Liam learned to surf. "There's always a swell at Phillip Island, which is why I love it there," he says of the island. "It's really small, it's kind of a little summer beach town, so I spent a lot of time surfing there with my brothers."

What he would say now to himself aged 17: "You are not cool. At all. Don't think you are, don't try to be. You're just not cool." At 17, the only thing I was concerned about was surfing. I had no real worries or cares in my life. I just surfed and thought I was cool."

YOUNG LOVE

Once Liam had moved to Phillip Island, he joined a local school, and it was there he met the girl who would be his first girlfriend. In an interview with Australian magazine *Woman's Day*, Laura Griffin told how she met Liam when he started school. "He was the new boy," she said, "and he was popular and made me laugh." It was clear that Liam was one of the most popular boys in the class. And it was at school that Liam decided he wanted to be like his older brothers... and become an actor.

"I've always loved surfing. When I was in school that was pretty much all that mattered in my life. Most of my friends surfed so we would go before school, after school, literally whenever we could."

making it

While Liam was still at school, older brothers Luke and Chris were already carving out careers as actors. Luke had appeared in Australian TV series *Blue Heelers*, *Last Man Standing* and the soap *Neighbours*, while Chris (who had also had a brief role in *Neighbours*) had acted in *The Saddle Club* and *Marshall Law* before winning a role in rival Aussie soap *Home And Away*, as Kim Hyde.

Although they are now both successful actors, Liam says he and his brother Chris aren't really rivals. "We are brothers and we are always competitive, but it's a good thing, it pushes us both and we are always happy whenever someone books something."

GETTING A BREAK

Seeing what his brothers were up to, Liam decided he wanted to give acting a try too. He hired an agent and started to look for acting roles. His first part came when he was just 17, a blink-and-you'll miss it part on *Home And Away* – his character doesn't even have a name!

It was a start, though. And Liam followed it with a one-episode appearance in the series *McLeod's Daughters*, a long-running drama set on a cattle station in the South Australian Outback. It was his next role, however, that would set him off on the road that would eventually lead to Hollywood…

EVERYBODY NEEDS GOOD NEIGHBOURS

While still at school, Liam auditioned for a role in the TV show that both his brothers had appeared in – *Neighbours*.

The series, which began back in 1985, is probably Australia's most famous TV show. The story of a collection of families who live on the Ramsay Street, Erinsborough, a fictional suburb of Melbourne; the daytime soap has run for over 6000 episodes and is shown in over 50 countries around the world.

Neighbours has featured a series of Australian actors early on in their careers who, like Liam, have since gone on to become international stars. Among the former *Neighbours* actors who have made it big are:

KYLIE MINOGUE – Launched a singing career after leaving *Neighbours* and has since had smash hits including 'Spinning Around', 'I Should Be So Lucky' and 'Can't Get You Out Of My Head'. She has an OBE for services to music.

JASON DONOVAN – A singer after he left *Neighbours*, Jason has won acclaim for his appearances in musicals including *Joseph And The Amazing Technicolour Dreamcoat*. He was one of the best contestants in 2011's *Strictly Come Dancing*, too.

GUY PEARCE – British-born Guy has appeared in a series of successful movies since leaving *Neighbours*, including *Memento*, *LA Confidential* and *The King's Speech*.

ALAN DALE – After leaving Australia, Dale won leading roles in *The OC*, *24*, *Lost* and *Ugly Betty*, as well as film roles in *Indiana Jones And The Kingdom Of The Crystal Skull* and *The Girl With The Dragon Tattoo*.

NATALIE IMBRUGLIA –Natalie is best known for her hit single 'Torn', which won her an MTV award for Best New Artist. She also co-starred in the movie *Johnny English* and was one of the judges on *Australian X Factor*.

INTRODUCING JOSH!

The role Liam was given was that of Josh Taylor, a love interest for one of the show's favourite characters, Bridget Parker. It had been announced on 13 July 2007 – when Liam was still just 17 years old – that he was joining the cast, and his first appearance aired on Australian TV three months later, on 29 October.

Liam's character, Josh, was a paraplegic following a surfing accident before he moved to Erinsborough, and he met Bridget – who was paralysed on one side of her body after being hit by a car – at physiotherapy sessions at the local pool. The two began an on-off relationship that became tricky when Bridget realised she still had feelings for her ex, and poor Josh eventually ended up alone before leaving Erinsborough for good.

the Road to Hollywood

Liam was now just 18 years old, and already on his way. After a year strolling the sunny streets of Erinsborough in *Neighbours*, he accepted a role in another TV series, the children's show *The Elephant Princess*. It's the story of an ordinary girl who discovers she is actually the princess of a mystical Indian kingdom, and Liam played her boyfriend, Marcus. He followed this with a role in the far more adult drama *Satisfaction*.

Of course, like many actors, Liam really wanted to make movies. His first chance came along in 2008, when he was offered a role in the British-made thriller *Triangle*, co-starring fellow Aussie Melissa George. Set on a deserted ship, the movie was filmed off the coast of Australia, and featured Liam, Melissa, Rachel Carpani, Emma Lung and Michael Dorman stranded on the boat as strange things start to happen (the Triangle of the title refers to the spooky Bermuda Triangle).

ON THE BIG SCREEN

It was pretty scary stuff, and while the movie got great reviews, it wasn't a huge hit, but it was enough to bring young Liam to the attention of Hollywood agents and producers. He followed it with a brief appearance in the Nicolas Cage sci-fi movie *Knowing* in 2009, and then – aged just 19 – got the call to Hollywood he had been waiting for. Fresh out of school, Liam had been offered the chance to try out for some of the hottest roles in movies. But there was a challenge ahead... his brother Chris was ready to carve out a career in Los Angeles too. Was there room in Hollywood for two Hemsworths?

Watching his brother Chris got Liam interested in acting. "I saw my brother doing it," he says, "and I thought I could do it better!"

LIAM

LUKE

SAMANTHA
LUKE'S WIFE

CHRIS

LEONIE
MUM

CRAIG
DAD

LIAM V CHRIS — BATTLE OF THE BROTHERS

	LIAM	CHRIS
AGE	22	28
HEIGHT	6ft 3in	6ft 3in
FIRST TV ROLE	HOME AND AWAY	NEIGHBOURS
FIRST MOVIE ROLE	TRIANGLE	STAR TREK
FIRST LEADING ROLE	THE LAST SONG	THOR
COMING SOON	ARABIAN NIGHTS	THE AVENGERS

CHRIS ON LIAM:

"We have a healthy rivalry as brothers do with certain things, but probably more about the little stupid things. I've been doing it for ten years and he's been doing it for about three. But he's doing great, he's got a whole lot of talent."

When Hollywood called in 2009, Liam stepped on a plane and endured the 13-hour flight that took him from his Australian home to the city of Los Angeles. He arrived on a tourist visa, which meant he had just 90 days to find a job before he would have to go back home!

He had already auditioned from Australia, sending a tape for the action movie *The Expendables* that was to star Sylvester Stallone, Jason Statham, Bruce Willis and Arnold Schwarzenegger. "Sylvester Stallone phoned me up a couple of days after he saw the tape and offered me a role," Liam remembers. "I was about to go over to Los Angeles for that when the script was completely re-written and six characters were cut. Mine was one of them. That was a big kick in the guts."

JET-SETTER

Determined to make it in Los Angeles anyway, Liam flew over for other auditions. One of the first roles he was asked to audition for was the lead in the Marvel comic movie *Thor* – and Liam's brother Chris was asked to audition too! "I auditioned very early on and then I was out of the mix and he was in the mix," Chris says about auditioning alongside his younger brother.

Despite being up for the same juicy role, Liam and Chris worked together on the auditions at home. "Liam and I would run through the script together and try to work out what we thought Ken (director Kenneth Branagh) wanted. We're pretty competitive in everything else we do, as brothers are, but this tended to be a bit of a team effort."

HEAD TO HEAD

In the end, it was Chris, and not Liam, who won the role of *Thor*. Chris joked that he knew a way to cheer up his brother after he lost the part: "I'm going to get him a *Thor* action figure, and a ticket to the movie!"

Liam jokes about what he did when he learnt his big brother had won the role of Thor: "I punched him in the head! No, I'm happier for him to get it than someone else. My brother's playing Thor! That's so cool…"

LIAM ON CHRIS:
"He got big (for the role of Thor). He's a freak!"

LIAM'S AWARDS!

He may only have starred in three movies but Liam has already been nominated – and won – a few awards:

KIDS' CHOICE AWARDS AUSTRALIA

Liam and Miley Cyrus were nominated for Favourite Kiss in *The Last Song* and also Cutest Couple!

australians in film

YOUNG HOLLYWOOD AWARDS

Teenagers voted in these awards, and Liam won the Young Hollywood Breakthrough Of The Year award in 2010 for his role in *The Last Song*.

TEEN CHOICE AWARDS USA

Liam was nominated with Miley Cyrus in the categories Best Liplock, Best Dance and Best Chemistry for *The Last Song*. And Liam won the award for Breakout Male Actor, beating *Kick-Ass*'s Aaron Johnson, *Adventureland*'s Jessie Eisenberg and Logan Lerman from *Percy Jackson And The Lightning Thief*!

Congratulations Liam!

the Last Song

Happily, the same week that Chris heard he had won the role of Thor, Liam got an important phone call of his own. "Within one week – it was probably the biggest week of our lives – I booked a movie called *The Last Song*, Chris booked *Thor* and then he booked a movie called *Red Dawn*. That was three studio films between us, so it was a really, really happy week for us."

Liam had been in Los Angeles, staying in an apartment with brother Chris for just five weeks when the script for *The Last Song* popped through his letterbox. Based on a book by Nicholas Sparks, it's the story of a rebellious teenage girl named Ronnie who spends the summer at her father's beach house. It's there she meets local boy Will, and the pair fall in love. However, there's trouble on the horizon, as both Will and Ronnie's dad have secrets that will come out and change Ronnie's life forever…

Liam was offered the role of Will, with singer/actress Miley Cyrus playing Ronnie and Greg Kinnear appearing as Ronnie's dad. The first time Will appears in the movie is when Ronnie is walking along the beach and Will crashes into her while playing volleyball, spilling her milkshake all over her!

PLAYING THE GAME

While Liam is a keen surfer and sportsman, he had never played volleyball before – but that wasn't going to stop him from trying his best. "Before we started shooting the movie, they asked me 'do you play volleyball?' and I said, 'yeah, no problem.' And I turned up for the first day of volleyball practice and I was honestly really scared to shoot the volleyball part because it takes a lot of skills to play that game and I didn't have them at all. I said to Julie Anne (the director), 'I think we're going to need a double,' but it's hard to find someone as big as me!"

Liam's first scene in the movie not only had him pretending he was good at playing volleyball, it also involved him playing the game without his shirt on! "I got the role probably four weeks before we actually started shooting and I started training immediately. I've always been pretty energetic, I grew up surfing and I do a lot of boxing and kickboxing and stuff so I was already pretty fit. But for the movie I had a personal trainer six days a week."

Liam on winning the role in *The Last Song*: "I was 19 at the time. It's a big deal. I was really scared. The biggest thing in my mind was not succeeding. That would have been embarrassing."

IF YOU LIKE THE LAST SONG, WHY NOT TRY...

THE NOTEBOOK

Like *The Last Song*, *The Notebook* is based on a weepie novel by Nicholas Sparks. An old man tells an old woman in hospital the story of a summer romance in the 1940s between local boy Noah (Ryan Gosling) and rich society girl Allie (Rachel McAdams) that is tested when her parents intervene, and they are separated during the Second World War. When they are reunited a few years later, Allie is engaged to someone else and has to choose which man to be with – her teenage love or her fiancé.

A WALK TO REMEMBER

An adorable tear-jerker starring Mandy Moore as preacher's daughter Jamie, who is forced to work on an after school project with local bad boy Landon (Shane West), only to discover over time that he's a real sweetie underneath. But just when things are looking adorably romantic between the pair, Jamie develops a cough, and anyone who has ever seen a sad love story before will know that it's only going to get worse.

REMEMBER ME

Twilight's Robert Pattinson stars as Tyler, a rebellious, rich college kid in New York who falls for Ally, the daughter of a tough police officer. While their backgrounds are totally different, they have lots in common – he mourns his older brother who committed suicide, while her mum was murdered on a subway platform in front of her – in a movie that's as much a love letter to New York as it is as a romance.

DEAR JOHN

Soldier John (Channing Tatum) is home on two-week leave when he meets college student Savannah (Amanda Seyfried). The pair fall in love, and when John returns to the army, they write to each other and carry on their romance. However, following the attacks on September 11 in New York, John decided not to leave the army to be with Savannah, and the pair have to choose whether to wait for each other or look for love elsewhere.

CHARLIE ST CLOUD

Young Charlie (Zac Efron) mourns his younger brother Sam so much he sees his ghost and spends time each day playing catch with him. Having given up the chance of a sailing scholarship at University, it seems Charlie will always be stuck, grieving for his brother – until he meets a pretty sailor named Tess, and an ambulance worker who reveals that Charlie's ability to communicate with his dead brother is actually a gift.

Meet Miley Cyrus

As filming on *The Last Song* started in Savannah, Georgia, photos were leaked to the press from the set – of Miley Cyrus kissing her leading man, Liam. "Who's that boy Miley was kissing?" teen magazines wondered, and everyone thought Liam must be the 16-year-old Hannah Montana star's boyfriend, until it was revealed the kissing was actually a scene from the movie!

"I got a hot boy," Miley told E! Online in an interview, adding that Liam was "not bad to look at for the summer." It seemed that Liam and Miley were just kissing for the cameras, though Miley did joke that she had handpicked Liam for the role because he was so cute. "I said to Nicholas Sparks (who wrote the movie and the book on which it was based), 'I like animals, I like music, I like hot Australians!' That's what I tried to make him write into the book, so it was interesting. It worked out fine, and I owe Nicholas, big time!"

Liam, meanwhile, got the opportunity to work with an actress who – still only 16 when they were filming *The Last Song* – had grown up in the spotlight. The daughter of country singer Billy Ray Cyrus and his wife Tish, Miley was born on 23 November 1992 and given the name Destiny Hope. Her parents often called her by the nickname Smiley, which became Miley as she got older.

Miley grew up on a 500-acre farm in Tennessee, but the family moved to Canada in 2001 when she was eight years old, as her dad was filming a TV series there. It was there that Miley decided that she wanted to be an actress, and she took lessons while also making a brief appearance in her dad Billy Ray's show *Doc*. After following this with a role in the Tim Burton movie *Big Fish*, Miley heard that Disney was auditioning young girls for a new TV series called *Hannah Montana*.

HANNAH MONTANA

The show was about a young schoolgirl who led a secret life as a pop star. Miley sent in a tape as an audition for the role of the girl's best friend, but was asked to audition for the lead role. It wasn't long before the whole world knew who 14-year-old Miley Cyrus was, as Hannah Montana became a smash hit.

LIAM AND MILEY — REAL LIFE LOVE

When Liam and Miley met in the early summer of 2009, she
was a big TV star (it is estimated she is worth around $1 billion!)
with a successful singing career, and he was an Australian actor
who was taking on his first leading male role. Miley had already
been linked to young actor Tyler Posey when they were both just
10 years old, but her first proper relationship was with singer
Nick Jonas, who she dated for two years from the age of 13.

"From the first day we met, it was good. I didn't know how big a star she really was — I had seen the show a few times, but I had no idea how big Miley Cyrus was. I guess that was good because I didn't get nervous"

LOVE IS IN THE AIR?

After they broke up, she dated
model Justin Gaston, but they split
up shortly before filming on *The
Last Song* began. Meanwhile, it was
rumoured that Liam was no longer
with his long-term girlfriend Laura.
Could a romance between the two
co-stars be on the cards?

At first, Miley wasn't interested in
a new romance. "I was actually going
through a tough time," she said in an
interview in 2010. "Guys needed to
be out of my life for a little while
and I just wanted to focus on my
work." So what made Miley change
her mind? "I met him, and he opened
the door for me, and I was like, I
have been in L.A. for three years and
I don't think any guy has actually
opened the door for me. It wasn't
that he wanted the job. That's just
who he is. I was like, 'Wow, that is
super-impressive.' I actually turned to
the director and said, 'He's got the
job.' He's hot and he opened the
door. Excellent."

AWKWARD!

As filming started, Liam and Miley realised they were more than just workmates. "We started filming and at one point the chemistry was kind of awkward. I liked him a little bit, he liked me a little bit, but it was awkward," Miley said. "Then I was like, 'OK, just fake it.' [I said] 'Please just pretend you like me' and he was like 'I don't have to pretend. I really do like you.' [Then it was like] 'OK, you're going to be my boyfriend. Cool.' "

Miley and Liam kept their relationship secret from the press throughout filming, and only confessed they were a couple months later when they were interviewed about *The Last Song*.

LIAM ON MILEY

"She's got such a big heart and is just so open. We feel very strongly about each other."

MILEY ON LIAM

"Love makes you feel beautiful and makes you feel good about yourself. That's what Liam does to me."

Australian leading men

Liam (and, of course, older brother Chris) isn't the first Australian to hit the big time in Hollywood. Among the other Down Under stars that have made it big on the big screen are:

RUSSELL CROWE Can you believe that one of Australia's most famous actors, 47-year-old Russell had a brief role in *Neighbours* at the start of his career? He really did, complete with a quiff and dodgy stubble! Following some leading film roles in Australia, Russell then became known for his roles in *The Insider, Gladiator* and *A Beautiful Mind*, all of which earned him Oscar nominations (he won one – for *Gladiator*). Russell has since starred in movies such as *Robin Hood* and *The Next Three Days*.

RUSSELL CROWE   RYAN KWANTEN

RYAN KWANTEN Born in Sydney, 35-year-old Ryan began his acting career in Aussie soap *Home And Away*. Since moving to the US, he won the role of Jason Stackhouse in the cult TV series *True Blood*, and has also starred in the movie *Red Hill*. He also supplied one of the voices for *Legend Of The Guardians: The Owls Of Ga'Hoole*.

HUGH JACKMAN

MEL GIBSON

XAVIER SAMUEL

SAM WORTHINGTON

HUGH JACKMAN Singer and dancer Jackman started off in musical theatre, performing on Broadway and London's West End, but hit the big time when he was cast in *X-Men* in 1999 as Wolverine. Since then, he has appeared in the *X-Men* sequels and prequels, as well as *Van Helsing*, *Australia* with Nicole Kidman, and *Real Steel*, and he has also hosted the Oscars. Up next, he will play Jean Valjean in a movie version of *Les Miserables*.

MEL GIBSON Although he was born in New York, Mel grew up in Oz from the age of 12. He won the role of *Mad Max* when he was 23, and soon became one of Hollywood's most sought after actors, starring in movies ranging from action thriller *Lethal Weapon* to romantic drama *Forever Young*. He won an Oscar in 1995 for directing *Braveheart*, and was most recently seen in the comedy drama *The Beaver*.

XAVIER SAMUEL *Twilight* fans will know 28-year-old Xavier better as Riley, from the *Twilight Saga: Eclipse*, his first big Hollywood movie. The role won him an MTV Movie Award for Best Fight, and he has followed it up with roles in *Anonymous* and the wedding comedy *A Few Best Men*. He'll next star alongside fellow Aussie Sam Worthington in the surfing drama *Drift*.

SAM WORTHINGTON Born in Surrey, England, but raised in Perth, Western Australia from the age of just six months, Sam hit the big time when he was offered the lead role alongside Christian Bale in 2009's *Terminator: Salvation*. His next role was even bigger – the lead in the biggest movie of the year, *Avatar*. Since then, Sam has starred as Perseus in *Clash Of The Titans*, and will also star in the movie's follow-up, as well as in two sequels (coming in 2014 and 2015) of *Avatar*.

the
Hunger
Games

By the time *The Last Song* was released in cinemas in America in March 2010, Liam had become one of the most talked about young actors in Hollywood. He was offered the sought-after lead role of Ali Baba in a new movie version of *Arabian Nights*, and accepted it happily. "I'm really excited about that," he said as the movie was announced in 2010. "I love epic films, *Lord Of the Rings* and stuff like that. I love getting into the physical shape of the character and feeling like you're in their skin. And I love action movies as long as they have a good story and good characters."

Arabian Nights is planned for a cinema release in 2013 with Chuck Russell directing. He already had lots of experience making a big budget action blockbuster, having made *The Scorpion King*, and rumour has it that Liam will be joined by another actor used to working on smash hit movies – Oscar winner Anthony Hopkins (who costarred with Liam's brother Chris in *Thor!*)

Liam was in demand, and also won the lead role in a Vietnam War romantic drama named *AWOL*, that he filmed in 2011 for release in 2012. But there was one role he – and every other young male actor in Hollywood – wanted more than any other. Could Liam win a role in the hottest teen movie since the *Twilight* saga?

THE CHANCE OF A LIFETIME

First published in 2008, *The Hunger Games* was the first in a series of three teen novels written by Suzanne Collins about young girl Katniss Everdeen. It was quickly compared to the *Twilight* saga of books – mainly because Katniss has two young men in her life, Peeta and Gale, just as Bella has in the *Twilight* books.

Aside from the possible love triangle, *The Hunger Games* is very different from *Twilight*, but when a movie of the book (and its two sequels) was announced, it soon became clear that the lead roles of Katniss, Peeta and Gale could be life-changing for the three actors hired to play them, just as Kristen Stewart, Robert Pattinson and Taylor Lautner's careers had changed following the release of *Twilight*.

THE HUNGER GAMES V TWILIGHT

PUBLISHED ///////////	2008 ///////////	2005 ///////////
NO. OF BOOKS IN SAGA ///	3 ///////////////	4 //////////////
AUTHOR ///////////	SUZANNE COLLINS //	STEPHENIE MEYER/
FEMALE LEAD ///////////	KATNISS EVERDEEN /	BELLA SWAN /////
MALE LEADS ///////////	PEETA AND GALE ///	EDWARD AND JACOB

THE PLOT

Sometime in the future after an apocalypse, North America has become the country of Panem, and the people that live in its 12 districts are answerable to the government in the Capitol. Each year, one boy and one girl from each district, aged between 12 and 18, is forced by lottery to appear in the Hunger Games, an event shown on TV in which they have to fight each other to the death until only one contestant remains.

16-year-old Katniss lives in District 12, where she hunts in the woods for food to feed her family alongside childhood friend Gale. When her sister's name is revealed in the Hunger Games lottery, Katniss volunteers in her place and is joined by Peeta, a boy she knows from school. When they arrive in the Capitol to be presented on TV to the viewers, Peeta reveals he is secretly in love with Katniss, but she is unsure whether he is telling the truth or just making up a story for the cameras. And she isn't sure how she feels about him either, especially as she has secret feelings for Gale…

35/

the Hunger Games

THE MOVIE

Soon everyone was trying to guess who would win the roles of Katniss, Peeta and Gale. More than 30 actresses read for the role of Katniss, including Hailee Steinfeld, Abigail Breslin and Saoirse Ronan – all of whom have been nominated for Oscars – but in March 2011 it was announced that Jennifer Lawrence (herself an Oscar nominee for Best Actress in 2010 for her role in *Winter's Bone*) would play the lead. But who would play her leading men?

Young actors Alexander Ludwig, Hunter Parrish and Lucas Till were considered for the role of Peeta, while Robbie Amell and *The Wizard Of Waverly Place*'s David Henrie were among those suggested for Gale. Then, on April 20, 2011, Liam got the news he had been waiting for. While Josh Hutcherson was cast as Peeta, Liam had won the role of Gale!

All three of the cast were thrilled to appear in one of the most anticipated films of 2012, and appeared in a glossy photo shoot in *Vanity Fair* magazine to celebrate.

JENNIFER: "I knew it was going to be huge, and that's scary. I called my mom. She said, 'This is a script that you love, and you're thinking about not doing it because of the size of it?' And I [didn't] want to not do something because I'm scared, so I said yes. And I'm so happy that I did."

JOSH: "I had a great read-through, and then came back to do a test screening a few weeks later. I also hit it off with Jen — the chemistry between the two of us really worked. A couple of weeks went by where I couldn't say a single word about it . . . then I got the call. It still didn't even hit me, until I walked on set for the first day."

LIAM: "I'd heard about how popular the books were, but I wasn't quite aware of how dark and gritty the story was. It started me thinking and asking questions like, 'Could something like this actually happen to us one day?' When you think about the fast-growing popularity of reality TV today, and the crazy premise of many of the reality TV shows that are currently on the air, is it really that far off for us to consider something like this being possible? I think it's a mind-blowing thing to think about."

IN THE SPOTLIGHT

Accepting the role of Gale in *The Hunger Games* meant that Liam was suddenly thrust into the spotlight. In the US, the books have a huge following, so his casting meant he was suddenly mobbed by adoring fans – just like Taylor Lautner and Robert Pattinson had been from the moment their roles in the *Twilight* movies had been announced.

He also made instant friends with co-star Josh Hutcherson, probably the only person who would understand how mad things were getting. "Josh is a pretty charismatic dude. I listen to him talk a lot, and he's smart, he's funny – he could convince me to do anything!"

FRIENDS REUNITED

The pair had met before – Josh had worked with Liam's brother Chris on the movie *Red Dawn* – so Josh quickly got in contact with his pal when he heard they were going to be in *The Hunger Games* together. "I sent him a text: 'Dude, we have *The Hunger Games*! I'm so stoked, man, this is awesome!" Soon they were hanging out together in North Carolina, where the film was shot over six weeks in the summer. Liam was spotted without his usual blond hair, having dyed his mop black for the role of Gale.

By the time Liam and Josh appeared on the cover of *Entertainment Weekly* magazine in July 2011, fan excitement was at fever pitch. Director Gary Ross talked to the magazine about the casting of Liam. "On first glance he's such a hunk that it's easy to just sort of ascribe a hunk-like simplicity to him. But this is a phenomenally subtle actor." Josh, meanwhile, talked about his relationship off-screen with Liam – they get on so well that Josh brought his co-star to Kentucky to meet his family and try his grandmother's famous fried chicken! "I think it's going to blow people's minds when they see that Peeta and Gale are actually best friends in real life."

JENNIFER LAWRENCE

Jennifer Lawrence also raved about her co-stars, calling Josh "charming" and saying about Liam: "He's just a solid brick of muscle and you look at him and you're like, 'Oh, okay, great!' But he's got depth and he's interesting and at the same time he's natural and he flows."

THE HUNGER GAMES... AGAIN?

Joining Josh, Jennifer and Liam in the cast of *The Hunger Games* was an impressive group of Hollywood actors, including Woody Harrelson, Elizabeth Banks, Stanley Tucci, singer/actor Lenny Kravitz and screen legend Donald Sutherland. Even while the movie was still filming, it was the most talked about project in Hollywood, so it came as no surprise when the producers announced that a sequel, based on the second book *Catching Fire*, would be made ready for release around the world on November 22, 2013. This meant that Liam already knew one movie he would be filming in 2012, a year in which he would be very busy indeed...

LIAM'S BROTHER CHRIS ON THE PAIRING OF JOSH AND LIAM IN *THE HUNGER GAMES*:
"They know each other outside of this as well, and I couldn't be happier that they're working together, especially on a film like this which has such a fan base. People are very dedicated and passionate about it, and I think they can feel safe that [the filmmakers] have made the right choice."

2012...
and Beyond...

WRITTEN IN THE STARS

WHAT DO THE STARS HAVE IN STORE FOR LIAM?

LIAM IS A CAPRICORN, AND PEOPLE UNDER
THIS STAR SIGN ARE KNOWN FOR BEING:

PRACTICAL

DISCIPLINED

AMBITIOUS

PATIENT

HUMOROUS

... AND MAYBE A BIT MISERLY!

They are all good traits to have as Liam makes
his way through Hollywood. Often confident, calm
and hardworking, Capricorns are known for being
reliable (always good on a movie set) and – good
news for Miley! – they are also intensely loyal in
relationships, loving and faithful (awww).

WANT TO CATCH LIAM'S EYE?

Capricorns like dark colours, and their star sign stone is the black onyx, while the birthstone for January (when Liam was born) is the red stone garnet. So wear some red and black! Tell him a joke (Capricorns love humour), and have a snowdrop in your hair, as it's the flower for January!

Already starring in one of the hottest movies of 2012, Liam's name is now mentioned every time a new, exciting project was announced. As well as the upcoming release of *AWOL* and the filming of *Arabian Nights* and *The Hunger Games 2* to come, by the end of 2011 Liam had signed up for another major movie and was rumoured to be starring in at least three more. First, in September 2011 he got a call from Sylvester Stallone, who had wanted to cast Liam in his action movie *The Expendables*, to say there was a role for him in... *The Expendables 2!*

ACURA
THE OFFICIAL
VEHICLE OF
S.H.I.E.L.D.

"I DON'T KNOW IF I'M A HERO TO CHILDREN, BUT I'D LIKE TO BE. I'D LIKE TO BE A GOOD ROLE MODEL."

LIAM GIVES BACK

In his spare time, Liam is an ambassador for the Australian Children's Foundation, a charity set up to help children have a life free from abuse, violence and trauma. His brother Chris and actor Eric Bana are also ambassadors for the charity.

"I have the best parents you can have. They have worked in child protection for 20 years and have only ever given me encouragement and support," Liam said when he joined the charity in 2010. "The world is a scary enough place as it is for children. It is important that home should always be a safe place for them."

THE EXPENDABLES 2

Liam joined a very impressive cast of eighties and nineties action heroes for the shoot, which began a month later. As well as Stallone himself, the film features Jason Statham, Dolph Lundgren, Mickey Rourke, Arnold Schwarzenegger, Jean-Claude Van Damme and Bruce Willis, making Liam the youngest member of the cast. The men all came together to make the movie in October 2011, filming in Bulgaria, Russia, France and China until the end of the year.

The Expendables 2 wasn't the only movie Liam was asked to star in. In November 2011, he was tipped to play Bruce Willis's son in the fifth *Die Hard* movie, *A Good Day To Die Hard*, that will be released in 2013. The character of tough cop John McClane's son, John McClane Jr, appeared for a few minutes in the first *Die Hard* movie in 1988 (as a little boy) but wasn't in the movie's three sequels. Now a grown man, the role in the new movie would be much bigger, as the story has John traveling to Russia to help his son, who has been caught up in the prison escape of a Russian leader.

2012 AND BEYOND

Liam has also been tipped to star as the male lead in another movie based on a Young Adult novel – *Fallen* by Lauren Kate. It's the story of a young woman who falls for a boy at her school, not realizing he's actually a fallen angel who was cast out of heaven for siding with Lucifer himself.

And, if those movies don't keep him busy, he's also got *Timeless* (a science fiction drama about a widower who travels back in time to see his wife) and possibly *The Power Of The Dark Crystal*, a sequel to the classic fantasy movie *The Dark Crystal*. 2012 is certainly going to be busy!

PICTURE CREDITS

Getty: 4, 6, 8, 11, 12, 14, 15, 20, 21, 22, 26, 27, 30, 31, 33, 34, 35, 38, 39, 43, 47
Rex: 3, 12, 13, 16–17, 29, 35, 37, 40

ACKNOWLEDGEMENTS

Posy Edwards would like to thank Jo Berry, Jane Sturrock, Jillian Young,
Helen Ewing and Smith & Gilmour

First published in hardback in Great Britain in 2012 by
Orion Books
an imprint of the Orion Publishing Group Ltd
Orion House, 5 Upper St Martin's Lane,
London WC2H 9EA
An Hachette UK Company

10 9 8 7 6 5 4 3 2 1

A CIP catalogue record for this book is available
from the British Library.

ISBN: 978 1 4091 4377 2

Designed by Smith & Gilmour
Printed in Spain

www.orionbooks.co.uk